P9-DCQ-551

My Catholic Identity
The Marks of the Church (and More)

Reproducible Handouts for Junior High

Active Learning for Catholic Teens

Hi-Time✳Pflaum
Dayton, OH

My Catholic Identity
The Marks of the Church (and More)

Active Learning for Catholic Teens
Reproducible Handouts for Junior High

Activities by Susan C. Benson
Sue has worked in parishes of the Archdiocese of Milwaukee for 23 years, during which time she served as Director of Christian Formation and as a classroom teacher. Her master's degree in Education is from Cardinal Stritch University in Milwaukee. In addition to her work for Hi-Time*Pflaum, she has written for the Living Waters Religion Series (Tabor Publishing) and contributed to the Milwaukee archdiocesan Grade Specific Curriculum project for grades 1-8.

Cover design by Larissa Thompson

Interior design by Patricia Lynch

The Scripture quotations contained herein are from the *New Revised Standard Version of the Bible*: Catholic Edition, ©1993 and 1989 by the Division of Christian Education of the National Council of the Churches of Christ in the U.S.A. All rights reserved. Used by permission.

"Holy with the Help of the Spirit" excerpt from the English Translation of *Rite of Confirmation, 2nd Edition* ©1975, ICEL. All rights reserved. Used with permission.

This publication includes images from CorelDRAW®9 which are protected by the copyright laws of the U.S., Canada and elsewhere. Used under license.

©2001 Hi-Time*Pflaum, Dayton, OH 45449. All rights reserved. Photocopying of the material herein is permitted by the publisher for noncommercial use. The permission line must appear on each reproduced page. Any other type of reproduction, transmittal, storage, or retrieval, in any form or by any means, whether electronic or mechanical, including recording, is not permitted without the written consent of the publisher.

ISBN: 0-937997-92-7

Contents

The Trinity Is Revealed!

Name _____

Our God is revealed to us in three persons: the Father, the Son, and the Holy Spirit. This we call a mystery of our faith because it is something we cannot fully understand. It is important, however, for us to recognize that it is in knowing the Father, Son, and Holy Spirit that we will come to know God.

Use your Bible to look up Mark 1:9-11. The Trinity was revealed at this event. Fill in the blanks to complete the passage. Use the scrambled words on the map to help you.

In those days Jesus came from _____ of Galilee and was

_____ by _____ in the _____.

And just as he was coming up out of the water, he saw the

_____ torn apart and the _____ descending

like a _____ on him. And a _____ came

from heaven, "You are my Son, the _____; with you

I am well _____."

ceiov

danroJ

tipzedba

vedolBe

vesneah

irtipS

azNareth

desaelp

ohJn

voed

Can you name two prayers that express Catholics' belief in the Trinity?

_____

_____

Think about it!

• To whom do you pray?

• When you pray, do you have a particular image of God in your mind?

• Which member of the Trinity do you picture in your mind?

• What does this member of the Trinity look like to you?

• From where do you think this image comes?

©2001 Hi-Time*Pflaum, Dayton, OH 45449 (800-543-4383). Permission is granted by the publisher to reproduce this page for classroom use only.

Mother of Us All

Name _____

Catholics believe that Mary is the mother of God, the mother of Jesus, and the mother of the Church. Mary is a model for us. Her faith, trust, and love of God give us an example of how to live and respond to God's love.

Look up the following Scripture passages. Read about Mary's life and experiences. Next to each citation, write a sentence to describe a quality of Mary that you feel is exemplified in the story, and that you feel might inspire us to the faith and love that Mary showed.

Luke 1:26-38 _____

_____

Luke 2:1-20 _____

_____

Luke 2:41-51 _____

_____

John 2:1-11 _____

_____

John 19:25-27 _____

_____

Choose a quality of Mary's that you would like to most exhibit in your life. Write a paragraph describing how you could do this.

Ideas: humility, obedience, determination, compassion, love, faithfulness, trust, strength

©2001 Hi-Time*Pflaum, Dayton, OH 45449 (800-543-4383). Permission is granted by the publisher to reproduce this page for classroom use only.

Follow by Example

Name _____

The saints are people in the history of the Church who serve as role models for all Christians. The Church often prays to saints in the form of a litany. In a litany a phrase is repeated throughout the prayer.

Complete the litany below by decoding the names of the saints. Write the letter that comes in the alphabet just before each letter indicated.

 Saint BOESFX, the first apostle called by Jesus, pray for us.

_____

Saint FMJABCFUI TFUPO, wife, mother, sister, and founder of schools, pray for us.

_____

 Saint MVLF, apostle and physician, pray for us.

_____

Saint HBCSJFM, archangel and messenger, pray for us.

_____

 Saint OJDIPMBT, gift-giving bishop, pray for us.

_____

 Saint BVHVTUJOF, writer and scholar, pray for us.

_____

Saint NPOJDB, faith-filled mother, pray for us.

_____

 Saint KPTFQI, protector of families, pray for us.

_____

Saint DMBSF, prayerful and poor, friend of St. Francis, pray for us.

_____

 Saint NBSUJO PG UPVST, soldier, hermit, and bishop, pray for us.

_____

Think about it!

 Tell why a saint who is familiar to you would be a good example for people your age.

©2001 Hi-Time*Pflaum, Dayton, OH 45449 (800-543-4383). Permission is granted by the publisher to reproduce this page for classroom use only.

Rituals of Our Faith

Name _____

Sacraments are special celebrations that are part of the Church's liturgy. They allow us to share more fully in the life of God. The rituals described below are part of sacramental celebrations. Identify each ritual by naming the appropriate sacrament.

1. This sacrament bonds a man and a woman together as one. They state their commitment in a series of vows. The symbol of this commitment is a ring worn on the left hand.

   _____

2. In this sacrament, we confess the sins we have committed. We express our sorrow and God forgives us. A priest prays with us, suggests ways to atone for our sins, and gives us suggestions for living better lives.

   _____

3. A person is anointed with oil and receives the gifts of the Holy Spirit in this sacrament. This sacrament completes the Sacraments of Initiation. A favorite symbol for this sacrament is a dove.

   _____

4. A man makes a commitment to serve the church in this sacrament. A bishop lays his hands on the person and prays for special grace for him. A stole is one of the common symbols of this sacrament.

   _____

5. A person becomes a member of God's family in this sacrament. The person wears a white garment and water is poured over his or her head. Water, the white garment, a candle, and oil are the symbols for this sacrament.

   _____

6. This sacrament is central to our faith, where we remember Jesus' Last Supper. We believe that we are sharing in the actual body and blood of Jesus in the form of bread and wine.

   _____

7. This is a sacrament adminstered to anyone who is ill or in danger of death. Prayers in this sacrament focus on healing a person's spirit as well as a person's body. Oil and a prayer book are used.

   _____

List the sacraments you have received, and if possible, identify the dates of the first time you celebrated them.

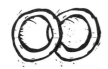

_____   _____

_____   _____

_____

©2001 Hi-Time*Pflaum, Dayton, OH 45449 (800-543-4383). Permission is granted by the publisher to reproduce this page for classroom use only.

Jesus' Gifts to Us

Name _____

The seven sacraments can be classified according to whether they are Sacraments of Initiation, of Healing, or of Mission. Write the names of the sacraments in the categories to which they belong.

Sacraments of Initiation

Through these three sacraments, Jesus enables believers to share the joy of his life with others in his Church.

_____   _____   _____

Sacraments of Healing

Through these two sacraments, Jesus continues his work as physician to heal our souls and bodies.

_____   _____

Sacraments of Mission

Through these sacraments, Jesus gives recipients the graces to work for the welfare and the salvation of others.

_____   _____

 ## Where in Scripture?

Each of the sacraments has its source in the Bible. Can you tell which sacrament is being referred to in each of these Scripture citations? Write its name on the line.

John 20:19-23   _____

Ephesians 5:25, 31-33   _____

John 3:5   _____

John 6:51,54,56   _____

Titus 1:5   _____

Acts 8:14-17   _____

James 5:14-15   _____

©2001 Hi-Time*Pflaum, Dayton, OH 45449 (800-543-4383). Permission is granted by the publisher to reproduce this page for classroom use only.

A Complete Change

Name _____

Catholics believe that Christ is made present in the bread and wine that becomes the Body and Blood of Christ. Solve this rebus to discover what we call this act of changing the substance of bread and wine into Christ's own Body and Blood.

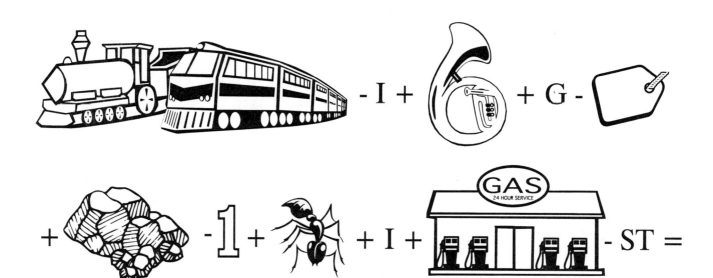

Do your work here:

_____

Answer:

_ _ _ _ _ _ _ _ _ _ _ _ _ _ _ _ _

©2001 Hi-Time*Pflaum, Dayton, OH 45449 (800-543-4383). Permission is granted by the publisher to reproduce this page for classroom use only.

United in the Eucharist

Name _____

The Mass is the central celebration of the Church and has drawn us together as a people since the time of Jesus. In it, Jesus is present in both his Word and in the Eucharist. The ritual we celebrate is similar to the ritual that the followers of Jesus experienced.

Number the parts of the Mass from 1-22 in the correct order.

Introductory Rites

____ Gloria

____ Opening Prayer

____ Gathering

____ Entrance Procession

____ Greeting

____ Penitential Rite

Liturgy of the Eucharist

____ Preparation of the Altar and Gifts

____ Sign of Peace

____ Lord's Prayer

____ Breaking of Bread

____ Communion

____ Eucharistic Prayer

Liturgy of the Word

____ Homily

____ Responsorial Psalm

____ First Reading

____ Second Reading

____ Creed

____ General Intercessions

____ Gospel Acclamation

____ Gospel

Concluding Rite

____ Blessing

____ Dismissal

As the gathered assembly, it is our privilege and responsibility to enter into worship to the best of our ability. Read the list below and check the ways you personally participate at Mass.

❏ Singing or responding at the appropriate time

❏ Listening attentively to the Scripture readings

❏ Singing in the choir

❏ Thinking about how God's Word relates to your life

❏ Serving at the altar

❏ Smiling and greeting others when arriving and leaving

❏ Reading along with the Gospel

❏ Fasting from food one hour before receiving communion

❏ Blessing yourself with holy water when entering and leaving

❏ Responding "Amen" after receiving communion

❏ Playing an instrument

❏ Living the values expressed in liturgy during the week

❏ Deciding how to serve others during the week

©2001 Hi-Time*Pflaum, Dayton, OH 45449 (800-543-4383). Permission is granted by the publisher to reproduce this page for classroom use only.

United in Many Ways

Name _____

A Creed is a statement of beliefs. The Creed we share as Catholics states that we are "One." This means that we are united with other Catholic Christians.

Below are examples of how many Catholic Christians are "One." Write the words or phrases under the correct headings.

• Teachings of Jesus • Celebration of the Eucharist • Jesus is God
• Celebration of Sacraments • prepare food for the hungry
• encyclicals • build homes for the homeless
• The Trinity • Liturgy of the Hours • magisterium
• support the missions • bishops
• Jesus rose from the dead
• Blessing Prayers • visit the sick
• priests • Jesus will come again
• Stations of the Cross
• care for the elderly • pope

Think about it!

Can you think of other ways we are united with other Catholic Christians?

©2001 Hi-Time*Pflaum, Dayton, OH 45449 (800-543-4383). Permission is granted by the publisher to reproduce this page for classroom use only.

Holy with the Help of the Spirit

Name _____

A creed is a statement of beliefs. The Creed we share as Catholics states that we are "holy." This means that the Holy Spirit helps the Church to be more like Christ.

We receive spiritual gifts at Baptism, which are strengthened at Confirmation. Below is a prayer from the Rite of Confirmation. Unscramble the words that name these spiritual gifts, and write them next to the correct meaning.

"Send your Holy Spirit upon them
to be their Helper and Guide.
Give them a spirit of wisdom and understanding,
the spirit of right judgment and courage,
the spirit of knowledge and reverence.
Fill them with the spirit of wonder and awe in your presence."

1. the ability to make good decisions

ritgh mentjudg _____

2. the strength to do what is right

caougre _____

3. seeing things from God's point of view

dosmwi _____

4. insight into the truths of the faith

gnidatsnrednu _____

5. discerning the truth

owledgekn _____

6. showing respect for God's creation

verreence _____

7. amazement at God's greatness

derwon/wae _____

©2001 Hi-Time*Pflaum, Dayton, OH 45449 (800-543-4383). Permission is granted by the publisher to reproduce this page for classroom use only.

Evidence of a Universal Church

Name _____

A creed is a statement of beliefs. Our Creed states that we are "catholic." This means that the church is universal. While respecting the cultures of each nation, the Church is visible throughout the world. Catholics strive to be present to all of humanity, living the Gospel by promoting peace and justice.

Read each statement below. Decode the location each statement refers to. Then find it on the map and indicate the correct letter.

A	B	C	D	E	F	G	H	I	J	K	L	M	N	O	P	Q	R	S	T	U	V	W	X	Y	Z
Z	Y	X	W	V	U	T	S	R	Q	P	O	N	M	L	K	J	I	H	G	F	E	D	C	B	A

1. _____ The Jesuit Refugee Service works in MZRILYR _____ to help refugees start small businesses.

   ✚ *Discuss: Why would the Church be interested in encouraging the world economy?*

2. _____ Catholic Charities USA helps residents in MLIGS XZILORMZ _____ _____recover from recent hurricanes.

   ✚ *Discuss: Why does the Church react to natural disasters, especially when government agencies often supply help?*

3. _____ Pax Christi, a world-wide Catholic peace organization, assists people in SZRGR _____with resources and education.

   ✚ *Discuss: Why does the Catholic Church promote peace education in small developing countries, instead of concentrating all efforts in large, powerful countries?*

4. _____ The St. Vincent dePaul Association gathers youth from around the world to meet in KZIRH _____to plan worldwide outreach efforts.

   ✚ *Discuss: Why is it important to engage youth in service to the world?*

5. _____ The Catholic Health Organization sends social workers to ILNZMRZ _____ to teach infant care skills.

   ✚ *Discuss: Why is the Catholic Church so actively involved in health care?*

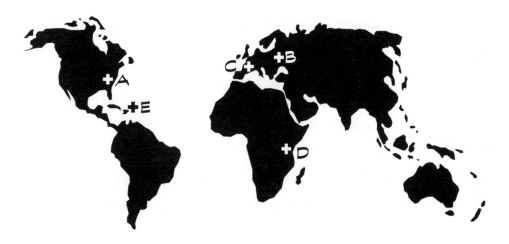

©2001 Hi-Time✳Pflaum, Dayton, OH 45449 (800-543-4383). Permission is granted by the publisher to reproduce this page for classroom use only.

The Apostles Are Our Guides

Name _____

Our Creed tells us that one of the marks of the Catholic Church is that it is "apostolic." This means that the teachings and traditions at the core of our faith today were passed down to us from the apostles.

We know the story of the early Church from reading the Acts of the Apostles. Use the Scripture citations for clues to answer the following questions.

1. The apostle who replaced Judas was _____.

   Acts 1:26

2. At Pentecost, the sound that identified the coming of the Holy Spirit is described as _____.

   Acts 2:2

3. Peter told the gathered community to repent and be baptized, and they would receive a gift. That gift was _____.

   Acts 2:38

4. The community dedicated themselves to the teachings of the apostles. They were dedicated to teaching, fellowship, prayer, and to the

   _____.

   Acts 2:42

5. Jesus was compared to something rejected by the builders. It was the

   _____.

   Acts 4:11

6. The early Christian community was described as being of one _____.

   Acts 4:32

7. An _____ led Peter and the apostles out of prison.

   Acts 5:19

8. The apostle Stephen was stoned to death. His last words were

   _____.

   Acts 7:60

9. Jesus' voice asked Saul, "Why do you persecute me?" when he was near the city of _____.

   Acts 9:3-4

10. There was a special Council to decide how much of the law of Moses new Christians must observe. This Council was held in the city of _____.

    Acts 15:2

©2001 Hi-Time*Pflaum, Dayton, OH 45449 (800-543-4383). Permission is granted by the publisher to reproduce this page for classroom use only.

Who Leads the Church?

Name _____

Church members who have been ordained in the sacrament of Holy Orders continue the ministry and leadership of the apostles. They are called deacons, priests, and bishops.

Many ordained ministers have led the Church well by word and example. Put the names of the people below on the timeline. Match the names with their descriptions.

John Neumann (1811-1860)   John Paul II (1920-)

John XXIII (1881-1963)   Oscar Romero (1917-1980)

1800   1900   2000

1. This pope declared Jubilee Year.

   _____

2. This pope called the Second Vatican Council. These meetings resulted in many significant reforms in the Church.

   _____

3. He was the archbishop of San Salvador. He worked to help the poor and suffering of his country in Central America. He was killed in while celebrating the Eucharist.

   _____

4. This saint was a bishop in Philadelphia who was known for organizing parishes and schools.

   _____

Write a paragraph about a priest you know, and tell how he has ministered to the Church.

_____

_____

_____

_____

_____

©2001 Hi-Time*Pflaum, Dayton, OH 45449 (800-543-4383). Permission is granted by the publisher to reproduce this page for classroom use only.

Employment Opportunities!

Name _____

Since the Second Vatican Council the role of the laity in serving the Church has been encouraged. Many roles have been developed for lay people to serve God and the Church. Some ministries are for life and require special training. Some are short-term commitments and require only willing hands and hearts.

Imagine you are writing for your parish bulletin. Choose three of these ministries and write a request for volunteers.

- lector • liturgy committee member • parish council member • server
- eucharistic minister • helper at meal program • nursing home visitor • fall/spring clean-up
- parish festival volunteer • catechist youth leader • parish newsletter editor

IMPORTANT

Serve one Sunday a month with our parish meal program. We will meet in the parking lot at 4:00 p.m. on the first Sunday of the month and car pool to the meal site. Call the parish office for details.

* * * * * * * * *

WANTED

MISSION

SPECIAL

Think about it!

Can you name other volunteer ministries at your parish?
Which ministry would you be most interested in participating in?

©2001 Hi-Time*Pflaum, Dayton, OH 45449 (800-543-4383). Permission is granted by the publisher to reproduce this page for classroom use only.

Who Is Your Role Model?

Name _____

The Communion of Saints is a spiritual union of all believers who form the body of Christ. These Christians, both living and deceased, can serve as role models in our daily lives.

Read the short descriptions of the Christians below.

Who was that handsome, well-dressed young man who got off the boat in Vera Cruz, Mexico in 1926? Was he a rich playboy or the man who broke the bank at Monte Carlo? Neither. He was Padre Miguel Pro, a recently ordained Jesuit priest back in his native Mexico, dressed in disguise. The Mexican government was violently anti-Catholic and eager to silence all priests. With a series of clever disguises, Father Pro eluded the police for over a year as he celebrated Mass and heard confessions. Finally captured, he faced a firing squad with the words, "Long live Christ the King" on his lips.

Jean Donovan was a lay missionary who ministered to the poor in El Salvador. She set up emergency services and taught religion. She was murdered by soldiers of the El Salvadorian army on December 2, 1980.

Johann Sebastian Bach (1685-1750) was a devout Lutheran who used his gifts as an organist and composer to praise God. He believed his music could lead people to greater devotion. His fans today still find that the nobility of Bach's music makes them more aware of the possibilities of the human spirit. He ended many of his compositions with the words, *Solo Deo Gloria*—"To God alone the Glory."

- Write about someone from history who can be a Christian role model.

  _____

  _____

  _____

- Write about someone you know today who would be a good role model for people your age.

  _____

  _____

  _____

©2001 Hi-Time*Pflaum, Dayton, OH 45449 (800-543-4383). Permission is granted by the publisher to reproduce this page for classroom use only.

Life Is a Gift

Name _____

```
T H E S E A R A E E E E T A L
L S I N S A B R S U S G E A I
K N S T T O E U T U H E R F I
F I T H R V B H B C O M R M A
N D D T E A A A M E N T O L M
W E I N G N L E V L W Y R X H
J O G U A O P F I G H T I N G
N E R S H P B X N J A G S Z P
P D I O E M P I P O T O M K D
R A C A I D U I T O R T U R E
X L D N M K I R N F E U Y B C
A P T G I Y Q C D G D Y Y R E
Z U U E E R I L I E J S Q L I
F I S R F U Y N G U R J K S D
S C A N D A L S B E S S V Q N
```

SEARCH WORDS

abortion

alcohol abuse

anger

drug abuse

euthanasia

fighting

hatred

kidnapping

murder

revenge

scandal

suicide

terrorism

torture

The first 41 unused letters give a hidden message. Write it here.

__ __ __ __ __ __   __ __ __   __ __ __

__ __ __ __ __ __   __ __ __ __   __ __ __

__ __ __ __ __ __   __ __ __ __ __ __ __ __ __ __.

©2001 Hi-Time*Pflaum, Dayton, OH 45449 (800-543-4383). Permission is granted by the publisher to reproduce this page for classroom use only.

An Ancient Practice

My Reflections on the Stations of the Cross

Jesus is condemned to death.
Have you ever been blamed for something you did not do? Write about how you felt.

Jesus takes his cross.
Have you ever had to do something very hard that you did not want to do? Write about how you got through it.

Jesus falls the first time.
Tell about a time that you were disappointed or feeling defeated. Compare your experience to how Jesus might have felt.

Name _____

Jesus dies on the cross.
Tell about the death of a person you knew.

Jesus is taken down from the cross.
Has anyone ever showed real care for you? Write about that experience.

Jesus is placed in the tomb.
We know that Jesus rose, but his three days in the tomb were a time of waiting. Describe the most difficult time you had to wait.

Draw your own symbol.

Jesus rises.
What is the most joyful time you have ever experienced?

Draw your own symbol.

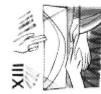

©2001 Hi-Time*Pflaum, Dayton, OH 45449 (800-543-4383). Permission is granted by the publisher to reproduce this page for classroom use only.

Jesus meets his mother.
How has your family supported you in difficult times?

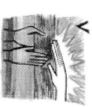

Simon takes Jesus' cross.
Have you ever helped someone in a special way? Was it difficult? Tell about it.

Veronica wipes Jesus' face.
Tell about a time a friend helped to make you feel better.

Jesus falls the second time.
Do you think you will have hard struggles in the future? What will your biggest challenge be?

Jesus speaks to the women.
What words of comfort would you give to someone who is feeling bad?

Jesus falls the third time.
What kinds of thoughts inspire you when you're feeling defeated?

Jesus is stripped of his garments.
Has anyone ever made fun of you? Write a short prayer expressing forgiveness of that person.

Jesus is nailed to the cross.
Have you ever been in pain? Describe your hurt. Think about the pain Jesus suffered.

©2001 Hi-Time*Pflaum, Dayton, OH 45449 (800-543-4383). Permission is granted by the publisher to reproduce this page for classroom use only.

Sacrament Matchups

Name _____

(page 1)

Sacramentals are objects and prayers of the Church that remind us of God's presence.

The following is a memory matching game to play with a partner. Cut apart the boxes and place them face down. Turn two cards over. If you match the name of a sacramental with its definition, you keep the pair. Try to collect more pairs than your partner does!

Prayer Beads	ROSARY
Blessed water, used to make the Sign of Cross	HOLY WATER
Cross with representative body of Jesus	CRUCIFIX
One dimensional rendering of a holy person	ICON
Candle blessed at Easter and used at celebration of the sacraments	PASCHAL CANDLE
Burnt fragrances used in worship	INCENSE

©2001 Hi-Time*Pflaum, Dayton, OH 45449 (800-543-4383). Permission is granted by the publisher to reproduce this page for classroom use only.

Sacrament Matchups

(page 2)

Name _____

Book of Scripture readings organized in three-year cycles		LECTIONARY
Book of official prayers for worship		SACRAMENTARY
Blessed oil used in the celebration of some sacraments		CHRISM
The cup used at Eucharistic liturgy		CHALICE
Renderings of the passion and death of Jesus		STATIONS OF THE CROSS
Place where Baptisms occur		BAPTISMAL FONT
Table for Eucharistic celebration		ALTAR

©2001 Hi-Time*Pflaum, Dayton, OH 45449 (800-543-4383). Permission is granted by the publisher to reproduce this page for classroom use only.

Remembering Mary

Name _____

The Rosary is a prayer that helps us to meditate on the events, or "mysteries" in the lives of Jesus and Mary. All but two of the mysteries appear in the Scriptures. Try to find a place in Scripture where the thirteen other mysteries occur. Write the Scripture citation next to each mystery.

Events, or Mysteries, of the Rosary

1. The Crowning of Mary
_____

2. The Resurrection
_____

3. The Crucifixion
_____

4. The Agony in the Garden
_____

5. Finding Jesus in the Temple
_____

6. The Annunciation
_____

7. The Visitation
_____

8. The Nativity
_____

9. The Scourging at the Pillar
_____

10. The Ascension
_____

11. The Crowning with Thorns
_____

12. The Descent of the Holy Spirit
_____

13. The Carrying of the Cross
_____

14. The Assumption of Mary
_____

15. The Presentation in the Temple
_____

See if you can place the mysteries in the proper categories.

Joyful Mysteries
__ __ __ __ __

Sorrowful Mysteries
__ __ __ __ __

Glorious Mysteries
__ __ __ __ __

The rosary beads represent the prayers HAIL MARY and OUR FATHER. Color the HAIL MARY beads blue and the OUR FATHER beads red.

©2001 Hi-Time*Pflaum, Dayton, OH 45449 (800-543-4383). Permission is granted by the publisher to reproduce this page for classroom use only.

The Church As an Artistic Expression of Faith

Name _____

Every place of worship has objects and furnishings to help people encounter the sacred. Catholic churches in particular have a long history of creating environments that enable private devotion as well as community prayer. Tour your own church and see what you can discover.

1. What are some of the objects in your church entrance that are welcoming? (a sign, bulletin board, plants, decorations, etc.)

2. Describe any statues inside or outside your church. Whom do the statues represent? What are they made of? Are they life-like or abstract?

3. Describe the Stations of the Cross in your church.

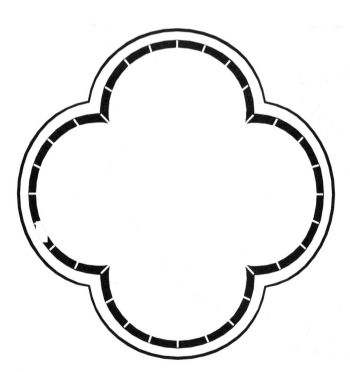

4. Describe any decorated or stained glass windows in your church. What do the designs resemble? Why do you think the artist designed them that way?

5. What other forms of art are used in your church? (mosaics, murals, tapestries, etc.) What do they show? How do they make you feel?

©2001 Hi-Time*Pflaum, Dayton, OH 45449 (800-543-4383). Permission is granted by the publisher to reproduce this page for classroom use only.

Seasons of Celebration

Name _____

We celebrate the seasons of the Church year in a yearly cycle. The seasons of the Church's liturgical year include Advent, Christmastime, Lent, Ordinary Time, Eastertime, and more Ordinary Time. There are also important feast days.

Look up the dates on this year's calendar for the feasts listed below. Then, write the following feasts and dates in their proper season. The cycle moves clockwise, beginning with Advent.

All Saints Day • Baptism of the Lord • Feast of St. Joseph • All Souls Day • Holy Thursday
Feast of the Holy Family • Epiphany • Assumption of Mary • Ascension of Jesus • Good Friday
Holy Saturday • Immaculate Conception • Easter Sunday
Can you add a few more?

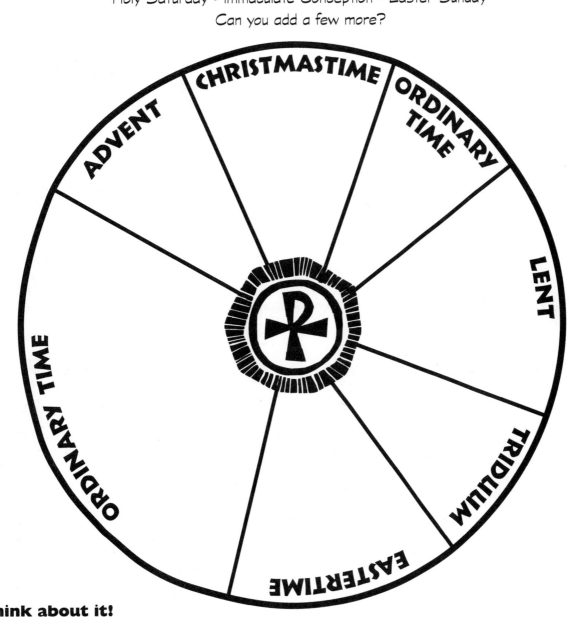

Think about it!

- What is your favorite liturgical season or feast?
- How does your family celebrate?

©2001 Hi-Time*Pflaum, Dayton, OH 45449 (800-543-4383). Permission is granted by the publisher to reproduce this page for classroom use only.

How Are We Alike?

Name _____

Because of disagreements throughout the history of the Church, Christians are separated into many denominations. Ecumenism is an effort to unite all Christians as well as to find common ground with other major religions.

Read the statements below. Decide which actions cause division and which can help move people toward unity.

1. Pray for unity.   Unite   Divide

2. Serve your community with people of other faith traditions.   Unite   Divide

3. Suppress curiosity about other faiths and traditions.   Unite   Divide

4. Hold prayer services with people from different religions.   Unite   Divide

5. Don't play sports with people of other religions.   Unite   Divide

6. Refuse to support the social justice efforts of other faiths.   Unite   Divide

7. Stay with your own kind and encourage others to do the same.   Unite   Divide

8. Keep quiet when classmates make fun of people of other faiths and cultures.   Unite   Divide

9. Take opportunities to learn about those different from yourself.   Unite   Divide

10. Expect people of other religions or cultures to dislike you.   Unite   Divide

Think about it!

Try to think of a few other ideas on how to promote unity with people of different cultures or religions.

©2001 Hi-Time*Pflaum, Dayton, OH 45449 (800-543-4383). Permission is granted by the publisher to reproduce this page for classroom use only.

Welcome!

Name _____

Evangelization is the activity of sharing the Good News of Jesus. Adults who are preparing to be baptized engage in a process called The Rite of Christian Initiation of Adults, or RCIA.

Match the stages of the process to their definitions. Then write the names for the stages in their correct order.

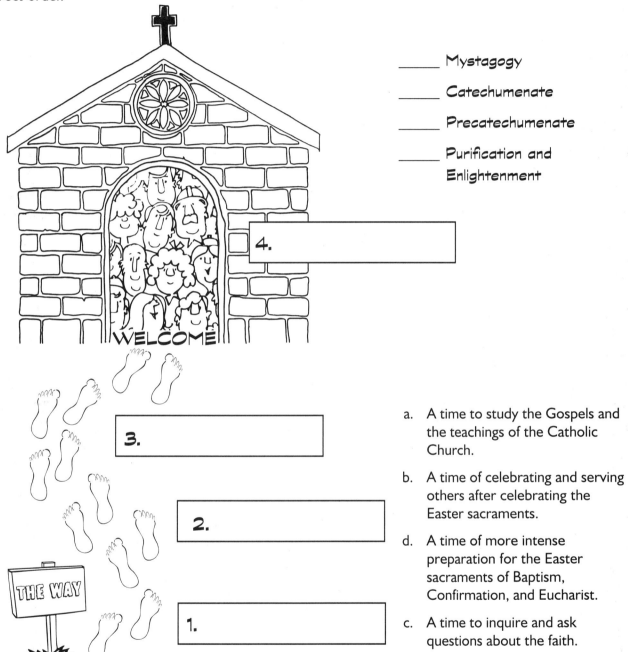

_____ Mystagogy

_____ Catechumenate

_____ Precatechumenate

_____ Purification and Enlightenment

4. _____

3. _____

2. _____

1. _____

a. A time to study the Gospels and the teachings of the Catholic Church.

b. A time of celebrating and serving others after celebrating the Easter sacraments.

d. A time of more intense preparation for the Easter sacraments of Baptism, Confirmation, and Eucharist.

c. A time to inquire and ask questions about the faith.

Think about it!
- Are there any adults or children preparing for the Sacraments of Initiation at your parish?
- How can you show your care and support?

©2001 Hi-Time*Pflaum, Dayton, OH 45449 (800-543-4383). Permission is granted by the publisher to reproduce this page for classroom use only.

Notes to Teacher

The Trinity Is Revealed
Nazareth; baptized; John; Jordan; heavens; Spirit; dove; voice; Beloved; pleased

Follow by Example
Andrew; Elizabeth Seton; Luke; Gabriel; Nicholas; Augustine; Monica; Joseph; Clare; Martin of Tours

Rituals of our Faith
Matrimony; Penance; Confirmation; Holy Orders; Baptism; Eucharist; Anointing of the Sick

Jesus' Gifts to Us
Initiation: Baptism, Confirmation, Eucharist
Healing: Penance and Anointing of the Sick
Mission: Holy Orders and Matrimony
Where in Scripture? Penance, Matrimony, Baptism, Eucharist, Holy Orders, Confirmation, Anointing of the Sick

A Complete Change
[TRAINS] - I + [TUBA] + G - [TAG] + [STONE] - [ONE] + [ANT] + I + [STATION] - ST = TRANSUBSTANTIATION

United in the Eucharist
Introductory Rites: 5,6,1,2,3,4
Liturgy of the Word: 12,8,7,9,13,14,10,11
Liturgy of the Eucharist: 15,18,17,19,20,16
Concluding Rite: 21,22

United in Many Ways
United in Belief: Teachings of Jesus; Jesus is God; Jesus rose from the dead; Jesus will come again; The Trinity
United in Worship: Liturgy of the Hours; Celebration of Eucharist; Celebration of sacraments; Blessing Prayers; Stations of the Cross
United in Leadership: encyclicals; magisterium; bishops; priests; pope
United in Service: prepare food for the hungry; build homes for the homeless; support the missions; visit the sick; care for the elderly

Holy with the Help of the Spirit
1. right judgment; 2. courage; 3. wisdom; 4. understanding; 5. knowledge; 6. reverence; 7. wonder and awe

Evidence of a Universal Church
1. Nairobi (D); 2. North Carolina (A); 3. Haiti (E); 4. Paris (C); 5. Romania (B)

The Apostles Are Our Guides
1. Matthias; 2. a violent wind; 3. the Holy Spirit; 4. breaking of the bread; 5. stone; 6. heart and soul; 7. angel; 8. Lord, do not hold this sin against them; 9. Damascus; 10. Jerusalem

Who Leads the Church?
1. John Paul II; 2. John XXIII; 3. Oscar Romero; 4. John Neumann

Life Is a Gift

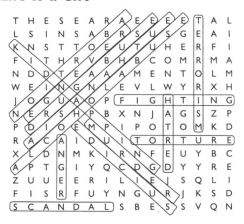

Unused letters: These are all sins against the Fifth Commandment.

An Ancient Practice
Photocopy activity back-to-back and fold into a booklet.

Remembering Mary
Joyful: 6,7,8,15,5
   The Annunciation: Lk 1:26-38
   The Visitation: Lk 1:39-45
   Nativity: Mt 1:18-2:2; Lk 2:1-7
   The Presentation in the Temple: Lk 2:22-24
   Finding Jesus in the Temple: Lk 2:41-46
Sorrowful: 4,9,11,13,3
   The Agony in the Garden: Mt 26:36-46; Mk 14:32-42; Lk 22:39-46
   The Scourging at the Pillar: Mt 26:67; Mk 15:15; Lk 22:63; Jn 19:3
   The Crowning with Thorns: Mt 27:29; Mk 15:17; Jn 19:2
   The Carrying of the Cross: Mt 27:32; Mk 15:21; Lk 23:26; Jn 19:17
   The Crucifixion: Mt 27:28-35; Mk 15:20-37; Lk 23:21-46; Jn 19:16-18
Glorious: 2,10,12,14,1
   The Resurrection: Mk 16:6; Lk 24:5; Mt 28:6; Jn 20:16
   The Ascension: Mk 16:19; Lk 24:51; Acts 1:9
   The Descent of the Holy Spirit: Acts 2:4
   The Assumption of Mary: none
   The Crowning of Mary: none

Welcome!
1. c. Precatechumenate; 2. a. Catechumenate; 3. d. Purification and Enlightenment; 4. b. Mystagogy